Paellas and Other

Spanish Rice Dishes

susaeta

Summary

RECIPES

Presentation

This recipe book offers you a detailed selection of the best paellas and rice dishes cooked in Spain. Although we have focused on traditional recipes, a special place has been set aside for new, different and surprising types of paella, which no doubt adds a fresh touch to the traditional recipe book.

The first news that we have about paella as a dish date back to the 16th century. In a treaty on Agriculture (recovered at the beginning of the 19th century), "Valencian-style Rice" is mentioned and, among others details, some of the dish's ingredients are given, such as rabbit or chicken. The same treaty says that at the time the dish was imitated in other areas of Spain. In other words, Valencian-style rice dishes were made in other parts of the Peninsula, just like today.

A couple of centuries later, in the 18th century, a reference to the "Valencian-style rice" appears in a recipe book, describing various theoretical aspects of its preparation, e.g. that the rice must be dry, and distinguishes between "Valencian rice" and "Catalan-style rice", two different ways of preparing it. Furthermore, the area's rice dishes began to have a place in various treaties, praising their quality.

Paella's international nature is nothing new, as since the 18th century many recipe books outside Spain mention it as one of the best rice dishes in the world. It is the case, for example, of Belgium, country where *riz à la valencienne* is a well-known dish.

Over time, other paella-based recipes have sprung up in various parts of the world, and the Conquest of America had a lot to do with it. In certain New World countries, they began to cook rice dishes, wishing to emulate the original Spanish paella, with varying success. Some of these dishes have reached our days and have their own name, as is the case of Colombian Paella, a recipe you'll find here in this book.

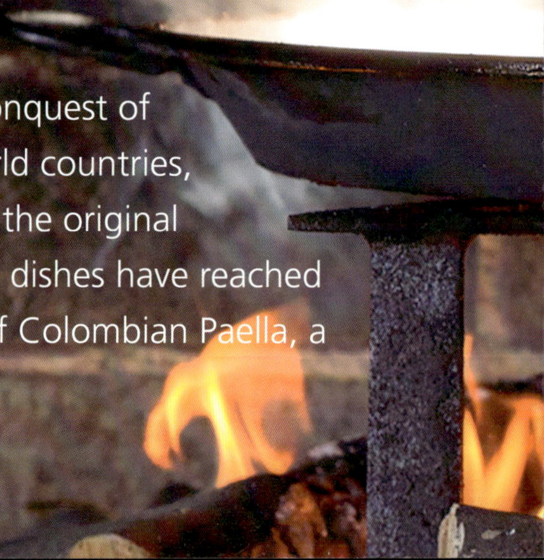

Traditional Paella

Few things can compare to a real paella prepared over a wood fire in a large paella pan, made with locally-produced vegetables and rice, at a cottage in the Spanish Levante region. A real paella requires these ingredients to be enjoyed as it befits,to pay a fitting tribute to such a traditional dish that definesthe soul of the Mediterranean people so well.

In the early days, the paella was cooked in an earthenware dish, a method used for a long time, as it was not until well into the nineteenth century that cooking utensils made of metal - preferably iron- were used in middle-class kitchens. And when they did, only the wealthiest had them, because not everyone could afford to buy pans, pots, and other vessels made of metal. Thus, little by little, iron replaced clay, the former being more resistant and durable than the latter. Kitchens in the Spanish Levante area showed their preference for a round type of pot, slightly deeper than the traditional paella pan, in which families would cook many different stews.

It was probably some members of the Valencian *Gremi de Ferrers* (Guild of Blacksmiths) who discovered the advantages of creating a *paella* (this word in itself meaning "pan", from the Latin *patella*) that was big enough to feed a group of friends or relatives; made of iron instead of clay; with two (or more) handles instead of one (like frying pans), to be able to transport it better, and a depth that allowed the rice to cook evenly and in less time than in the typical earthenware dishes. Also, the paella pan could support the high temperatures of the direct flames from the wood fire, as well as the blows it would certainly receive in the labourers' carts, when being taken to work.

Thus, paella and the paella pan are of rural origin, associated with the fields along the Mediterranean coast. The pan would be placed over small fires, where various vegetables and meats were cooked and then rice and water or stock added. When the rice was ready, the paella would be eaten with wooden spoons directly from the pan, without using plates. Besides being a delicious dish, it was also a form of socializing and sharing with friends and family.

The first ingredients came from the marshes -eels and snails - and from the Levante fields - green beans, butter beans, etc.-. Later, when the economy allowed, and poultry was no longer a luxury product, chicken and rabbit were introduced. Rice, as well as saffron – also brought to us by the Moors -, came from the surrounding farmlands.

Valencian Paella

La Albufera witnessed the birth of the real Valencian paella. Fertile land like few others, this rice-growing area near the lagoon has centuries of tradition, which led to this cereal becoming and still being a staple part of the Valencian diet. If we add the shortage of cattle in favour of poultry breeding and fertile fields, the result is logical: paella.

While there are many rice dishes cooked in a paella pan along the Mediterranean coast, there can be no doubt that the Valencian paella is the benchmark of this dish, today an international one. For this reason, the Valencian Community Department of Agriculture, together with the Valencian Rice Designation of Origin Regulatory Council, has published a list of the ingredients that all paellas should include if they wish to use the Valencia "hallmark", namely: chicken, rabbit, green beans (*ferraura*), butter beans (*garrofón*), tomato, rice, olive oil, water, saffron and salt. These would be the basic ingredients, which, according to the Community of Valencia area where it is made, one or more of these other ingredients would be added: garlic, artichoke, duck, paprika, snails or rosemary.

Although paella originally included these ingredients, in time, a wide variety of others have been introduced. The proximity of the coast, fertile fields and the import of more or less exotic products, have brought variety and novelty: mixed paella that includes shellfish and fish with poultry, fish paella, shellfish paella, vegetable paella... There are plenty of varieties to choose from and increasingly more chefs who create new versions of this delicious dish.

Butter beans
Chicken
Artichoke
Green beans
Rice
Rabbit

Rice Stews & Creative Paellas

In addition to the traditional paella, where the rice should absorb all the liquid, we can't forget the wide variety of rice dishes made in a paella pan or in an earthenware dish and that are included in the rice recipes cooked in the Iberian Peninsula Mediterranean coast style, but whose result is a more or less soupy rice.

Especially on the Catalan coast, as well as in the Balearic Islands, we find a series of rice dishes that are a gastronomic benchmark of these areas. In general, they usually contain more seafood than traditional paella and it is very typical to combine them with inland produce, resulting in rice dishes that are usually known as being from "sea and mountain".

With the arrival of new culinary trends, paella has also adapted to the times and in many restaurants it is possible to taste "original" paellas, i.e. other forms of paella with innovative ingredients and very successful results. With the appearance of other types of rice on the gastronomic scene, for example long grain or wild, paella has changed, but is just as delicious.

Since it saw the light at a moment in history difficult to specify (just as with any other dish), paella has become the most famous dish in popular cuisine not only Valencian, but also Spanish, and has a legion of admirers who associate it with our beaches and our endless sun. Certainly, not all paellas and rice dishes served at restaurants in our country can boast their quality, but many are those who seek to ensure its name is not discredited and continue cooking the rice in the traditional way, naturally and using quality ingredients. With this book, we try to add our grain of sand to contribute to this mission.

The Best Types of Rice

Today in any supermarket you can find different types of rice. However, not just any rice will do for making paella or rice stew, so we must choose the right one for each recipe. Furthermore, although this may seem unimportant at first, the quality of the grain has a lot to do with the final result, as we explain below.

Rice started being grown approximately 7,000 years ago in the South of China, but did not come to Valencia, the area of the Iberian Peninsula where it was planted for the first time, until the 8th century A.D. It was specifically on the shores of the Albufera lagoon, in Sueca, where the first paddy was planted. Between the late 19th and early 20th centuries the rice paddies we know today were finally planted.

The technique used to grow rice consisted of extracting the soil from the centre of the lagoon and depositing it on the shores in order to achieve the ideal soil for growing rice. The suitability of this soil produced, and continues to produce, utmost quality rice.

The Valencian Designation of Origin (D.O.) protects the rice produced in Valencia, specifically La Albufera rice fields and the Pego-Oliva marshes, where the Japonica, Senia, Bahia, Albufera and Bomba varieties, among others, are grown. Due to their traditional cultivation in these lands and their organoleptic characteristics, three of them are protected by this Designation of Origin: Senia, Bomba and Albufera. Below, we will explain what is special about each of them in the preparation of paella and rice dishes.

The *Bomba* variety is perhaps the best known and the most appropriate for making certain rice dishes. In addition to the Valencia Rice D.O., it is also protected by the Calasparra Rice D.O. It is more expensive than other types of rice because the hectare of crop yields less than others, but it is worth it, as it is very rich in amylose (a starch component), which has a very important feature: it does not overcook, it is always loose, while you expose it to prolonged cooking. It therefore has a creamy texture, and absorbs the aromas and flavours superbly.

While the *Senia* variety is less known, it is very similar to Bomba and many are those who even believe it is of a higher quality than the latter. It is a round-grain rice, so the flavours are absorbed well. However, as a result of this it often goes soggy easily, so it is more frequently used by the more experienced paella cooks.

Within the Bomba variety, we find a sub variety called *Albufera*. This round-grain rice is a cross between the Bomba and Senia varieties. An excellent quality and also protected by the Valencia Rice D.O., this type is particularly suitable for preparing paellas and rice stews.

In addition to these three Valencia Rice D.O. varieties, which are also the most often employed, there are other rices with Designation of Origin grown in the rest of Spain and that are ideal for making the recipes in this book. One of them is the Delta de Ebro Rice D.O. comprising the Bahia, Senia, Sequial and Tebre varieties. In this land, rice-growing has a long tradition, dating back, as in the case of Valencia, to the time of the Arabs, thus indicating the quality of this product. On the other hand, Calasparra Rice D.O. varieties include rices from the Calasparra and Moratalla regions, in Murcia, once again in the Spanish Levante. This designation includes the Bomba and Balilla x varieties, both white and brown, all of them superior quality.

Tips for Preparing Perfect Paella

Although each paella cook has their own secrets, oddities and habits, a series of essential rules must be taken into account for making perfect paella. Below we give you some tips that guarantee - only if you follow them step-by-step- that our paellas will never disappoint.

1. Quality of the ingredients

As in any good dish, and more in this case if possible, it is necessary to use highest quality ingredients. First you have to choose the rice well, because it's the main ingredient: whichever kind it is, it's preferable to spend a little more and be sure to buy a good rice. The economic difference in many cases is minimal, but the final result can vary a lot. For both paellas and rice stews, the best are the round-grain Senia, Bomba or Bahia rice varieties. You must also take into account that you should use a good extra virgin olive oil, fresh vegetables and meats, and quality shellfish or fish. And, of course, it is better to use homemade stocks.

2. Utensils

The paella pan must be wide and its size will depend on the number of diners. It must also be low, as paella rice needs to cook in a thin layer. So, it is always best to use a large round paella pan rather than cook more rice than fits into the pan. The spoons used for stirring the ingredients must be wooden; for large paellas, a kind of shovel with a long handle (also wooden) is frequently used. The ideal thing is to cook the paella over a wood fire, but if a gas hob is used, it is necessary to use a diffuser, since the heat must be evenly distributed throughout the whole paella pan.

3. Cooking Times

This is a question of experience, as there are so many factors involved in cooking rice. As a general rule, on reaching simmering point, it should cook for 18-20 minutes (10 minutes on high and the rest on low), but the times vary according to the hob; just try, try and try again...

4. Proportions

We usually use 100 g of rice per person, but this amount can vary: if you use a lot of meat, vegetables, etc., then you'll need less rice, but if you're using just a few ingredients, it's possible that this amount needs to be increased to up to 150 g per person. The right amount of olive oil should used: generally about 300 ml of oil per kilo of rice, but make sure you don't use too much as the rice will go soggy. As for the liquid (either water or stock), the ideal proportion is 2.5 litres per kilo of rice, but it also depends on the hob heat: if it's very high, it will require a little more liquid, because it will evaporate more quickly.

5. Tips

Although there is diversity of opinion in this regard, some people prefer to sauté the rice before adding the liquid so the grain will "seal" - the most superficial layer is slightly sealed by the oil, which makes it harder for the rice to overcook. Never wash rice used to make paella; if you do, you'll be removing the starch, an essential component for the paella's creamy texture. Use natural saffron and avoid using artificial food colouring.

Traditional Paellas

Mixed Paella

Ingredients:

FOR 6 PEOPLE
DIFFICULTY: MEDIUM
TIME: 1 HOUR AND 30 MINUTES

500 g rice
500 g chicken meat
150 g lean pork
100 g diced Serrano ham
50 g fresh peas
1 l water
12 mussels
12 clams
4 prawns
1 medium squid
2 artichokes
2 tomatoes
2 cloves of garlic
1 green pepper
½ red pepper
extra virgin olive oil
a few strands of saffron
paprika
parsley
salt

Preparation:

1. Dice the chicken and pork.
2. Wash the peppers, remove seeds and cut into pieces. Peel and chop the garlic and tomatoes. Wash the artichokes and remove leaves, leaving only the hearts.
3. Clean the squid and cut into slices.
4. Put a pan of water onto the hob and when it boils, add the peas and artichoke hearts and cook for 10 minutes on a high heat. Once cooked, strain and set aside. Cut the artichoke hearts into four pieces.
5. Put a paella pan on the hob with a dash of oil and, when hot, fry the chicken and pork for 5 minutes on a high heat. Add the ham, and once everything is sautéed, remove from the pan and set aside.
6. In the same oil, fry the pepper, garlic and tomato. Stir and cook for 2 or 3 minutes and add the artichoke hearts. Cook, stirring all the time, for 3 or more minutes.
7. Add the squid, season with paprika and stir well.
8. Add the rice and prawns. Finally, add the peas and parsley. Sauté everything.
9. Put a pan with water on the hob and bring it to the boil.
10. Add the mussels and clams, the meats and hot water to the paella pan.
11. Cook until the rice is ready, approximately 20 minutes. Check the seasoning and add a few strands of saffron. Take off heat.
12. Let the paella stand for 5 minutes off the hob before serving.

Tuna & **Shellfish** Paella

Ingredients:

FOR 6 PEOPLE
DIFFICULTY: LOW
TIME: 1 HOUR AND 10 MINUTES

500 g rice
300 g fresh prawns
300 g squid
300 g clams
1.5 l water
1 fish stock cube
8 mussels
200 g tuna steak
2 tomatoes
1 onion
1 red pepper
2 cloves of garlic
extra virgin olive oil
a few strands of saffron
1 sprig of parsley
salt

Preparation:

1. Dice the tuna steak. Put a large pan of salted water on to boil. When it starts boiling, add the prawns and tuna. Simmer slowly for 10 minutes.
2. Wash the mussels and clams thoroughly and add them to the pan. Wait until they open and, when most of the shells open, take the pan off the heat and discard the closed ones. Strain the stock well and set aside. Shell the clams and peel the prawns; set aside in a bowl
3. Peel the tomatoes and chop them together with the pepper and onion.
4. Wash and chop up the squid.
5. Put a pan on the heat with a little oil and, when hot, sauté the tomato, the pepper and onion 2 or 3 minutes. Then add the rice and squid, lightly brown, and add the stock from cooking the shellfish and tuna. Crumble in the stock cube and a few strands of saffron. Cook over a low heat for 20 minutes, stirring occasionally.
6. Meanwhile, peel the garlic and mash with the parsley. 5 minutes before the rice is ready, add it to the pan along with the clams and the prawns. Stir well.
7. When the rice is cooked, take the pan off the heat and arrange the mussels carefully.Cover the paella pan with a cloth. Leave to stand for 10 minutes and garnish with chopped parsley before serving.

Hake Paella

Ingredients:

FOR 6 PEOPLE
DIFFICULTY: LOW
TIME: 1 HOUR

500 g rice
1 l fish stock
1 kg hake
2 tablespoons of homemade tomato sauce
1 red pepper
1 onion
1 clove of garlic
extra virgin olive oil
salt

Preparation:

1. Boil the fish stock in a pan. Keep it warm over low heat.
2. Peel and chop the onion and garlic. Wash the pepper and chop it into small pieces. Wash and slice the hake.
3. Put a paella pan on the heat with a dash of oil and, when hot, sauté the onion, garlic and pepper. When the vegetables are soft, add the hake and cook all together for about 5 minutes on a medium heat. Then remove the hake and set it aside.
4. Add the tomato sauce to pan, stir well and pour in the fish stock. Leave to cook for 5 minutes over a medium heat.
5. Add the rice by scattering it over the surface of the pan, and cook for 15 minutes. Stir from time to time, making sure you don't run out of stock. If necessary, add a little water.
6. Finally, 5 minutes before the rice is fully cooked, put the hake back in. Correct the seasoning if necessary, and cover pan.
7. Turn off the heat and let the paella finish cooking with the residual heat.
8. Take the pan off the heat and leave to stand 5 minutes more before serving.

Norway Lobster Paella

Ingredients:

FOR 6 PEOPLE
DIFFICULTY: LOW
TIME: 1 HOUR AND 15 MINUTES

500 g rice
800 ml water
1 kg Norway lobsters
4 ripe tomatoes
4 cloves of garlic
1 chili pepper
extra virgin olive oil
salt

Preparación:

1. Mash the unpeeled garlic cloves and the chili pepper in a mortar.
2. Peel the tomatoes, chop them and set aside in a bowl.
3. Put a paella pan on the heat with a dash of oil and, when hot, add the lobsters, a little salt and the garlic sauce and chili pepper; stir well and sauté for 5 minutes.
4. After this time, put the lobsters on the sides of the pan, and put the tomato in the hole left in the centre. Season again, mix and lightly fry without stirring.
5. Once the tomato is fried, add about 800 ml of water, and from the moment it starts to boil, let it simmer for 10 minutes.
6. After this time, remove the lobsters one by one with the help of tongs and set aside.
7. Add the rice to the paella pan and cook for 8 minutes on a high heat, then 10 minutes on a low heat, and 5 minutes on a high heat again so the rice will be loose and dry. Stir occasionally to prevent it from sticking.
8. About 3 minutes before the end of cooking, add the lobsters and stir everything very welll Remove from heat and serve.

Traditional Valencian Paella

Ingredients:

FOR 6 PEOPLE
DIFFICULTY: MEDIUM
TIME: 1 HOUR AND 10 MINUTES

600 g rice
½ rabbit
750 g chicken
500 g green beans
250 g butter beans (garrofon)
3 artichokes
150 ml tomato purée
3 sprigs of rosemary
a few strands of saffron
extra virgin olive oil
water
salt

Preparation:

1. Dice the chicken and rabbit.
2. Wash the artichokes and green beans. Remove the hardest leaves from the artichokes and cut hearts into four. Chop the beans.
3. Put a paella pan on the heat with a dash of oil and, when hot, add the chicken and rabbit, Add salt and cook for 5 to 10 minutes. Once brown, put the pieces on the sides of the paella pan.
4. Put the artichoke hearts, the green beans and the butter beans in the middle. Add salt, stir and let the vegetables simmer on a low heat for approximately 10 minutes.
5. Add the tomato purée and a few strands of saffron, mix well, and cover all ingredients with water.
6. Boil for 15 minutes and, when the water has evaporated a little, scatter in the rice (forming a cross, i.e. dividing the pan into four). Season with rosemary and cook until the water has been absorbed, about 20 minutes more.
7. Remove the pan from the heat, cover with a cloth and et the rice rest 5 minutes before serving.

Note

It is said that there are as many paella recipes as people who make it. This is the typical Valencian Paella recipe and it is made using the most representative ingredients of this traditional dish. However, variations can be introduced according to personal taste. Valencian Paella did not used to be served on plates, but was eaten directly from the pan.

Seafood Paella

Ingredients:

FOR 6 PEOPLE
DIFFICULTY: MEDIUM
TIME: 1 HOUR AND 10 MINUTES

500 g rice
1 l fish stock
100 g King prawns
100 g prawns
100 g small clams
100 g mussels
100 g of squid rings
4 cloves of garlic
2 ripe tomatoes
2 green peppers
extra virgin olive oil
a few strands of saffron
salt

Preparation:

1. Soak the clams in a bowl with water and salt for about 20 minutes so they will release the sand; drain and set aside.
2. Meanwhile, put a pan with a little water on the heat, and when it begins to boil, add the mussels and cook until they open. Once ready, take the pan off the heat, strain the liquid well and set aside.
3. Cook the King prawns and prawns and peel them.
4. Wipe the squid rings with a cloth.
5. Heat the fish stock in a saucepan and keep it warm over low heat.
6. Peel and chop the garlic cloves. Wash the tomatoes and peppers and chop them finely.
7. Heat oil in a paella pan and then add the garlic, tomato and pepper and sauté over a medium heat during 5 minutes, stirring all the time. Then add the squid rings and clams. When the clams open, pour in the fish stock and the liquid from cooking the mussels.
8. Once the stock starts to boil, add the rice, a few strands of saffron and salt to taste.
9. Cook for 10 minutes over a high heat and then 6 minutes more over a low heat. 5 minutes before the rice is fully cooked, decorate the paella with the King prawns, prawns and mussels. Wait for it to finish cooking.
10. Take the pan off the heat, cover with a cloth and let it stand 5 minutes before serving.

Prawn & Clam Paella

Ingredients:

FOR 6 PEOPLE
DIFFICULTY: LOW
TIME: 50 MINUTES

500 g rice
300 g prawns
250 g clams
1 l fish stock
200 ml white wine
½ onion
extra virgin olive oil
a few strands of saffron
pepper
salt

Preparation:

1. Peel the prawns and wash the clams thoroughly. Set aside.
2. Pour the wine into a bowl and add a few strands of saffron and a pinch of pepper.
3. Peel and chop the onion.
4. Heat a little oil in the paella pan on the hob, then add the onion and cook it over a low heat for 10 minutes, or until soft. When ready, add and sauté the rice, then pour in the fish stock.
5. When the stock starts to boil, add the saffron-infused wine. Stir, and cook for 20 minutes, or until the rice is tender.
6. About 5 minutes before it is fully cooked, add the prawns and clams, check seasoning, and add salt if necessary.
7. Once it is fully cooked, take the pan off the heat, cover with a cloth and wait 10 minutes before serving.

Note

Prawns and clams are the perfect couple of ingredients for making a simple but very tasty and aromatic paella. If you don't have fresh prawns, which is ideal, you can always use frozen, but make sure they are good-quality. As for the clams, it is always advisable to let them soak in salted water for 20 minutes to release the sand they contain, but this step is not necessary if they are good-quality, especially when you haven't much time and need to prepare a quick meal.

Valencian Paella
with Rabbit and Snails

Ingredients:

FOR 4 PEOPLE
DIFFICULTY: MEDIUM
TIME: 1 HOUR (PLUS MACERATION TIME)

400 g Bomba rice
500 g clean snails
½ rabbit
500 g chicken
2 tomatoes
a few strands of saffron
2 bay leaves
1 sprig of thyme
1 sprig of rosemary
1 green pepper
2 cloves of garlic
2 large dried peppers (ñoras)
150 ml extra virgin olive oil
1 l water
ground black pepper
salt

Preparation:

1. Clean the chicken and rabbit and cut into small pieces. Put both in a bowl and season with salt and pepper. Add the very finely-chopped cloves of garlic, rosemary, thyme and one bay leaf, stir well, cover the bowl and marinate in the refrigerator for 2 hours.
2. Put the snails in a pan with plenty of water and cook for 10 minutes. Drain and return them to the pan with clean water and the other bay leaf. Cook for 20 minutes. Once cooked, drain and set aside.
3. Wash the peppers, remove seeds, chop and set aside. Peel and chop the tomatoes and set aside. Soak the dried peppers in water.
4. Once macerated, put a paella pan with oil on the heat and fry the chicken and rabbit pieces for 15 minutes until golden. Remove the pieces of meat and set aside.
5. Add the pepper, tomato, saffron and the meat from the dried peppers. Sauté over a medium heat for 5 minutes.
6. Add the meat and snails. Stir, add the rice and a pinch of salt. Cook for 1 minute while stirring, and add the water.
7. Cook the rice on a high heat for 5 minutes; then reduce to medium and cook for 15 minutes more.
8. Leave to stand 5 minutes before serving.

Fish Paella

Ingredients:

FOR 6 PEOPLE
DIFFICULTY: MEDIUM
TIME: 1 HOUR AND 10 MINUTES

500 g rice
200 g conger eel
200 g monkfish
200 g cuttlefish
1.5 l water
12 mussels
12 prawns
1 tomato
a few strands of saffron
extra virgin olive oil
salt

Preparation:

1. Clean the conger eel and monkfish, chop the squid into small pieces and clean the mussels.
2. Wash and peel the tomato, remove seeds and chop it.
3. Put a pan with water on the heat and, when it boils, add the conger, Monkfish and mussels and cook for 20 minutes. Strain and set aside the stock and fish separately.
4. Put a paella pan on the heat with a dash of oil and, when hot, fry the prawns and squid for 5 minutes over a medium heat. Then add the rice, tomato, a few strands of saffron and a pinch of salt, and stir for 3 to 5 minutes, until the rice "seals".
5. Pour in the fish stock and continue cooking for 20 minutes more. When half-ready, add the fish and mussels and lower the heat.
6. When the rice is ready, take the paella pan off the heat, cover with a cloth and wait 5 minutes before serving.

Note

The sea offers us many treasures that, besides tasting delicious, have many nutritional benefits. A clear example of this are mussels, a mollusk available all year round and with a high protein content.

Rabbit Paella

Ingredients:

FOR 6 PEOPLE
DIFFICULTY: MEDIUM
TIME: 1 HOUR (PLUS MACERATION TIME)

500 g rice
1 medium rabbit
1 ripe medium tomato
1 onion
2 cloves of garlic
extra virgin olive oil
1 tablespoon of thyme
1 tablespoon rosemary
1 tablespoon cumin
a few strands of saffron
ground black pepper
sweet paprika
salt

Preparation:

1. Chop the rabbit and place in a bowl; add salt, black pepper, half a teaspoon of thyme and half a teaspoon of rosemary. Mix well and leave to marinate overnight in the refrigerator.
2. Peel and chop the onion. Peel and slice the garlic. Peel the tomatoes, remove seeds and chop.
3. Put a paella pan on the heat with oil, and when it is hot, add the rabbit and fry well; remove and set aside.
4. Add the onion, sliced garlic and tomato to the paella pan and sauté over a low heat for 10 minutes, stirring occasionally, until the sauce thickens and is dark. Take the paella pan off the heat and set aside.
5. Put the rabbit in a pot and cover with water. Bring to the boil and cook for 20 minutes on a medium heat. Add the rest of spices: thyme, cumin and rosemary. Stir. When the rabbit is cooked, remove from the heat and set aside.
6. Put the paella pan back on the heat and add a pinch of paprika, pepper and a few strands of saffron, and stir vigorously. Next, pour the contents of the pot, including the boiling stock, up to the height of the paella pan rivets. Salt to taste.
7. Add the rice and cook 5 minutes on a high heat and another 10 minutes on medium. If the stock starts to evaporate too much, lower the heat. Stir.
8. When is the rice ready, remove from the heat and let it stand for 5 minutes before serving.

King Prawn & **Squid** Paella

Ingredients:

FOR 6 PEOPLE
DIFFICULTY: LOW
TIME: 1 HOUR

500 g rice
300 g King prawns
300 g squid rings
300 g clams
2 tomatoes
4 cloves of garlic
1 red pepper
1 green pepper
½ cup of white wine
1 l water
extra virgin olive oil
sweet paprika
a few strands of saffron
salt

Preparation:

1. Wash the peppers, remove the seeds and chop. Peel the garlic and tomatoes and chop finely.
2. Put a paella pan on the heat with a generous dash of oil and, when hot, sauté the peppers 5 minutes over a medium heat.
3. Add the tomatoes and garlic, and sauté until everything is well done, about 10 minutes more.
4. Add the prawns, squid rings, clams and wine. Season with paprika and a pinch of salt.
5. Stir, cover the pan and leave to cook for about 8 minutes.
6. After this time, uncover pan and add the rice, water and a few strands of saffron. Stir again so the rice is well coated and cook for about 20 minutes, until the liquid is absorbed.
7. The paella is nearly ready when it is creamy, not soupy. That's why it is better to wait until the rice sticks a little to the bottom of the pan, but it should never be allowed to get completely dry.
8. Take the paella off the heat and serve.

Vegetable Paella

Ingredients:

FOR 6 PEOPLE
DIFFICULTY: LOW
TIME: 50 MINUTES

500 g rice
300 g green beans
300 g carrots
300 g artichoke
300 g of tomatoes
1 l water
1 onion
1 small can of red peppers
extra virgin olive oil
a few strands of saffron
salt

Preparation:

1. Peel and finely chop the onion. Peel the carrots and cut them into sticks. Wash beans and cut in not very small pieces. Clean the artichokes and chop them. Wash, peel and chop tomatoes. Cut into peppers into strips.
2. Put a pan on the heat with a dash of oil and, when hot, fry the onion for 5 minutes. Then add and sauté all the vegetables, except the tomato and peppers, for 10 minutes over a low heat. Then add the tomato. Add salt and continue cooking, stirring occasionally until the vegetables are cooked.
3. Meanwhile, put a pan on the heat with the water and bring to the boil.
4. Once the sauce is ready, add the rice, stir for a few minutes and add the boiling water and some strands of saffron threads. Cook over a low heat for 20 minutes, stirring occasionally.
5. 5 minutes before it is ready, decorate with peppers. Check the seasoning and correct if necessary.

Note

Artichokes have many minerals, vitamins and antioxidants. They also contain a good amount of fibre, carbohydrates, proteins and small amounts of fatty acids. Artichokes have always been a prized food, already eaten by Greeks and Romans. During the Middle Ages, it was introduced in England by King Henry VII, subsequently crossing the English Channel, and Catherine de Medici became one of its most fervent devotees.Due to their high price, only the wealthiest could afford to eat artichokes.

Creative Paellas

Quail Paella

Ingredients:

FOR 6 PEOPLE
DIFFICULTY: LOW
TIME: 50 MINUTES

500 g rice
6 quail
1 l water
½ onion
1 green pepper
1 red pepper
2 tomatoes
extra virgin olive oil
a few strands of saffron
salt

Preparation:

1. Clean the quails well and chop them.
2. Wash the peppers, remove seeds and cut up. Wash and cut up the tomatoes. Peel and finely chop the onion.
3. Place paella pan on heat with a dash of oil and, when hot, fry the quails for 5 minutes over a medium heat. Remove the meat from the pan and set aside.
4. Sauté the onion in the same oil for 5 minutes. When brown, add the peppers and tomatoes, and continue sautéing over a low heat for 10 minutes, stirring occasionally.
5. Add the rice and water. Cook for 5 minutes on high and then reduce to low and simmer for 15 minutes more. 5 minutes before the rice is fully cooked, add the quail, a few strands of saffron and salt. Stir.
6. When the water has been absorbed, take the paella pan off the heat and leave to stand 5 minutes before serving.

Note

This tasty and wholesome paella can be made with a wide variety of other meats if you don't have quail: chicken, rabbit, pork, veal or any other game birds, such as pigeon or partridge.

Port Wine & **Shellfish** Paella

Ingredients:

FOR 6 PEOPLE
DIFFICULTY: MEDIUM
TIME: 1 HOUR

500 g Bomba rice
1 l fish stock
4 Norway lobsters
12 King prawns
12 mussels
12 clams
200 g squid rings
1 onion
1 green pepper
1 red pepper
2 tablespoons homemade tomato sauce
Port wine
extra virgin olive oil
salt

Preparation:

1. Peel the onion, clean the peppers and chop everything.
2. Put a frying pan on the heat with a dash of olive oil, and when it is hot, add the chopped vegetables; add salt and sauté over a medium heat for 5 minutes. Turn off the heat and set aside.
3. Put a saucepan on to heat the fish stock, and keep it warm over a low heat.
4. Meanwhile, place a paella pan on the heat with a dash of oil and, once it is hot, add the squid rings. When they start to brown, add the prawns, mussels, clams and lobsters, and sauté for 10 minutes over a low heat, stirring from time to time.
5. When the shellfish is brown, add a good dash of Port and let it be absorbed. Then add the sautéed vegetables, stir everything well, and add the fish stock and tomato sauce. Check seasoning and stir again.
6. Add the rice and cook over a gentle heat for 20 minutes. If 10 minutes after cooking the stock has been nearly absorbed, you can add more. Correct the seasoning if necessary.
7. Remove the paella pan from the heat and leave to stand for 5 minutes before serving.

Note

The production of Bomba rice, considered one of the best in the world, is limited due to the delicate and intense care required for growing it. It is the round-grain rice preferred by rice experts, because of its excellent texture qualities that mean it is always just right.

Pepper Paella

Ingredients:

FOR 6 PEOPLE
DIFFICULTY: LOW
TIME: 45 MINUTES

500 g rice

1 l fish stock

1 large red pepper

2 green peppers

½ onion

extra virgin olive oil

a few strands of saffron

salt

Preparation:

1. Peel the onion, clean the peppers and cut all into thin shreds.
2. Put a saucepan on to heat the fish stock. Keep it warm for later use.
3. Place a paella pan on the heat with a dash of oil, and when hot, add the onion, peppers and salt. Sauté over a medium heat for about 5 minutes, or until the vegetables are soft and the onions start to brown.
4. Add the rice and toss a few seconds, stirring all the time before pouring in the hot fish stock. Also add some strands of saffron. Adjust the seasoning if necessary
5. Cook the paella for approximately 20 minutes, or until the grain is tender and the stock has evaporated. At this point, set aside the paella pan and cover it with a cloth.
6. Leave to stand for 10 minutes before serving.

Note

Peppers are a source of very important health benefits. They have a high content in vitamin C and vitamin B6, essential for the proper functioning of both of the brain and the central nervous system.

Tomato & **Prawn** Paella

Ingredients:

FOR 6 PEOPLE
DIFFICULTY: LOW
TIME: 45 MINUTES

500 g rice
150 g crushed tomatoes
200 g peeled prawns
½ onion
½ green pepper
½ red pepper
extra virgin olive oil
water
pepper
salt

Preparation:

1. Peel and finely chop the onion. Clean and chop the peppers.
2. Put a paella pan on the heat with a dash of oil and when hot, sauté the onion and peppers until soft. Then, add the tomato,and sauté until the sauce has evaporated slightly.
3. Add six cups of water to the pan and, when it starts to boil, add the rice, salt and pepper. Cook for 20 minutes or until the rice is tender. About 5 minutes before it is ready, add the prawns and continue to cook until the rice is completely ready.
4. Take the paella off the heat and leave for 5 minutes before serving.

Note

Red prawns (also known as pink prawns) have interesting nutritional properties, being low in fat and with a high content of iodine, a mineral beneficial for the good functioning of the metabolism. In addition, the iodine in red prawns helps to regulate cholesterol, as well as the processing of carbohydrates and strengthens hair, skin and nails.

Real Paella

Ingredients:

FOR 6 PEOPLE
DIFFICULTY: LOW
TIME: 50 MINUTES

500 g rice
200 g green beans
300 g chicken breast
1 l chicken stock
1 onion
1 clove of garlic
1 green pepper
1 red pepper
a few strands of saffron
extra virgin olive oil
pepper
salt

Preparation:

1. Peel and chop the onion. Wash the green beans thoroughly and the peppers well, and cut up.
2. Dice the chicken breast.
3. Place a paella pan on the heat with a dash of oil and sauté the onions, adding a pinch of salt and pepper; stir. Add the other vegetables so they brown together with the onion. After 5 minutes, add the clove of garlic, peeled and crushed, and a few strands of saffron; stir.
4. Add the chicken and brown it. Then add the rice and sauté everything, without stirring too much, for 10 minutes over a low heat.
5. Then pour the chicken stock over the paella and cook over a medium heat for 15 minutes and then on a high heat for 5 minutes more.
6. Remove the pan from the heat and leave to stand 5 to 10 minutes before serving.

Octopus & **Mushroom** Paella

Ingredients:

FOR 6 PEOPLE
DIFFICULTY: LOW
TIME: 45 MINUTES

500 g Bomba rice
300 g boiled octopus
1 l fish or shellfish stock
100 g mushrooms
½ onion
½ red pepper
extra virgin olive oil
paprika
a few strands of saffron
turmeric
fresh parsley
salt

Preparation:

1. Peel the onion, clean the pepper and mushrooms, and cut up. Finely chop the parsley.
2. Put a paella pan on the heat with a dash of oil and, when hot, add the onion and pepper, and sauté over a medium heat. After 5 minutes, add the mushrooms and sauté them for 2 minutes more.
3. Add the octopus and toss it the right time to cook it, but taking care not to overcook. When it is nearly cooked, add the rice and stir.
4. Now add the stock and season with parsley, paprika, saffron, turmeric and salt. Let the rice simmer over a medium heat for 20 minutes.
5. After this time, remove the paella from the heat, cover it with a cloth and let it rest for 5 minutes before serving.

Note

Octopus is a delicious marine cephalopod mollusk with a unique flavour and aroma, as well as highly versatile. Although in Spain the traditional way of serving it is in vinaigrette or Galician-style (with olive oil, paprika and a little salt), this paella recipe is an easy and very tasty way to enjoy it.

Pork Ribs & **Clam** Paella

Ingredients:

FOR 6 PEOPLE
DIFFICULTY: LOW
TIME: 1 HOUR AND 15 MINUTES

500 g rice

250 g pork ribs, in small pieces

500 g clams

1 l water

1 onion

2 green peppers

2 artichokes

½ head garlic

extra virgin olive oil

a few strands of saffron

thyme

pepper

salt

Preparation:

1. Preheat the oven to 180 ° C.
2. Put a saucepan with water on the heat and, when it begins to boil, put in the clams. Cook them for 20 minutes over a medium heat. Remove from heat and set aside (keeping the liquid).
3. Peel and chop the garlic and the onion. Clean and chop the peppers. Remove the toughest leaves from the artichokes and cut into quarters.
4. Put a paella pan on the heat with a dash of olive oil and fry the ribs for 10 minutes over a low heat. Once fried, remove from pan and set aside.
5. In the same oil, fry the garlic and, once golden, add the onion, pepper and artichokes. Sauté over a low heat for 10 or 15 minutes.
6. Once the sauce is ready, add the ribs, the rice and cook over a low heat for 5 minutes without stirring.
7. Pour in the liquid (previously strained) from cooking the clams and the clams; season with salt, pepper, saffron and a little thyme and when it starts to simmer, take the pan off the heat and put it in the oven.
8. Bake the paella in the oven for 20 minutes.
9. When the stock has been absorbed, take out of the oven and leave to stand for 5 minutes before serving.

Cod & Vegetable Paella

Ingredients:

FOR 6 PEOPLE
DIFFICULTY: MEDIUM
TIME: 1 HOUR AND 20 MINUTES

500 g rice
5 large artichokes
200 g cauliflower
250 g desalted cod
1 fish stock cube
1 tomato
1 clove of garlic
the juice of 1 lemon
extra virgin olive oil
a few strands of saffron
sweet paprika
water
salt

Preparation:

1. Fill a bowl with water and add the lemon juice.Clean the artichokes, removing the hardest leaves and cut the hearts into quarters; soak them in the lemon water.
2. Cut the cauliflower into small pieces and add to the bowl with the artichokes.
3. Put a pan on the heat with the content of the bowl, including the liquid, and cook for 20 minutes once it starts to boil. When vegetables are ready, drain and set aside.
4. Crumble the cod and set aside in a bowl. Peel and slice the garlic. Peel the tomato and puree it using a food mill.
5. Put a paella pan on the heat with enough oil to cover the base. When it starts to heat up, add the garlic slices, and once they start to brown, add the tomato. Stir for 10 minutes and then add a pinch of paprika and stir with a slotted spoon to avoid burning.
6. Add the cauliflower and artichokes, a few strands of saffron and cover everything with water. Crumble in the fish stock cube and stir. When the stock has been boiling for 1 minute, taste, and correct the seasoning, if necessary. Add the rice and spread it out with slotted spoon; cook on a high heat for 5 minutes.
7. Lower the heat to medium and add the cod; cook for 5 minutes. Check how much stock is left and, depending on the amount, raise or lower the heat to prevent the rice from drying before reaching 15 minutes total cooking time.
8. Remove from the heat and let the paella stand for 5 minutes covered with a cloth before serving.

Peasant's Paella

Ingredients:

FOR 6 PEOPLE
DIFFICULTY: LOW
TIME: 1 HOUR

500 g rice
500 g cabbage
200 g onion
50 g bacon
100 g lean pork
250 ml chicken stock
1 l water
extra virgin olive oil
parsley
pepper
salt

Preparation:

1. Medium-dice the meat and set aside.
2. Peel and chop the onion. Remove the cabbage leaves and slice into very fine shreds.
3. Place a large paella pan on the heat with oil and, when it is hot, fry the meat. Remove meat from the paella pan and set aside.
4. Sauté the onions in the oil and, when it is transparent, add the bacon; toss for about 5 minutes over a medium heat.
5. Add the cabbage and cook for 15 minutes until soft, stirring occasionally.
6. At the end of this time, add the rice and meat to the paella pan, and cook for 2 minutes. Then pour in the stock and water, stir well and bring to the boil.
7. Add salt and pepper to taste and cook for 15 minutes. Once the rice is ready, sprinkle with chopped parsley and remove the pan from the heat.
8. Leave to stand 5 minutes before serving.

Colombian Paella

Ingredients:

FOR 6 PEOPLE
DIFFICULTY: MEDIUM
TIME: 1 HOUR

500 g rice
2 chicken breasts
200 g mussels
150 g squid rings
300 g shrimps
400 g Norway lobster
150 g peas
700 ml water
1 carrot
1 red pepper
1 tomato
1 onion
2 cloves of garlic
4 bay leaves
olive oil
turmeric
pepper
salt

Preparation:

1. Peel the onion, garlic and carrots, and chop finely. Clean and chop the peppers. Peel the tomato and purée it in a food mill. Meanwhile, cut up the chicken breasts, and season with salt and pepper.
2. Cook peas in boiling salted water 5 minutes.
3. Place a paella pan on the heat with a dash of oil and, when hot, add the onion and garlic; sauté for 3 minutes, stirring frequently. Then add the carrot, pepper and tomato, and continue cooking over a medium heat for 10 minutes, stirring from time to time.
4. Meanwhile, put a frying pan on the heat with a dash of oil and, when it is hot, fry the chicken over a medium heat for about 5 minutes. When it is ready, add it to the paella pan and stir so it will soak in the taste of the vegetables.
5. Add the rice, water and mussels. Stir until the mussels open and discard the ones that are closed. Then, add the squid rings, shrimps and lobsters.
6. When all the ingredients are in the paella pan, cook for 5 minutes over a high heat and then lower the heat again until the water begins to boil. Then add the bay leaf and season with salt, turmeric and pepper.
7. Stir so that the rice is well coated and then cook for 15 minutes or until the water has evaporated. After about 10 minutes, add the peas and mix.
8. Take the paella pan off the heat and leave to stand for 5 minutes before serving.

Wild Rice Paella

Ingredients:

FOR 6 PEOPLE
DIFFICULTY: LOW
TIME: 40 MINUTES (PLUS MACERATION TIME)

500 g wild rice
250 g pine nuts
250 g raisins
1 l water
1 onion
200 ml brandy
extra virgin olive oil
salt

Preparation:

1. Let the raisins and pine nuts macerate in brandy for 1 hour.
2. After this time, drain the raisins and pine nuts. Set aside.
3. Peel and chop the onion.
4. Put a paella pan on the heat with a dash of oil and, when hot, add the onion and sauté over a medium heat for 5 minutes, stirring frequently.
5. Add the rice and fry lightly, stirring constantly, for 3 minutes. Then, add salt to taste and pour in the water; leave to cook over a medium heat for 15 minutes.
6. After this time, add the raisins and pine nuts and continue cooking 5 minutes more over a low heat, with the paella pan covered.
7. When the rice is ready (it must be completely dry), take the pan off the heat, stir well and serve immediately.

Note

Despite its name, strictly speaking wild rice should not be classified as a rice, because it comes from a different plant called Zizania, and it is usually sold in supermarkets mixed with long rice, a product that we use in this recipe. It has a very high satiating power, because of its high fibre content. Therefore, it is perfect for those who want to watch their figure.

Mushroom Paella with Olives

Ingredients:

FOR 6 PEOPLE
DIFFICULTY: LOW
TIME: 40 MINUTES

500 g long grain rice
100 g black pitted olives
300 g mushrooms
1 tomato
4 cloves of garlic
extra virgin olive oil
a few strands of saffron
water
pepper
salt

Preparation:

1. Peel the garlic cloves and mash them in the mortar. Clean and slice the mushrooms.
2. Put a paella pan on the heat with oil and, when hot, sauté the mashed garlic 5 minutes over a high heat; when golden, add the peeled and chopped tomato, the mushrooms and the olives.
3. Sauté for 5 minutes and add salt and pepper.
4. When the sauce is ready, add the rice and fry lightly, Stirring all the time, for a couple of minutes.
5. Cover the rice with the water add the strands of saffron and cook over a medium heat for 20 minutes, until the rice is ready.
6. Remove the pan from the heat and leave the rice to stand 5 minutes before serving.

Long Rice Paella with **Hare**

Ingredients:

FOR 6 PEOPLE
DIFFICULTY: MEDIUM
TIME: 1 HOUR AND 15 MINUTES

500 g long grain rice
200 g hare
1 l chicken stock
1 onion
1 green pepper
1 tomato
extra virgin olive oil
ground black pepper
a few strands of saffron
salt

Preparation:

1. Peel and chop the onion. Wash the pepper, remove the seeds and chop. Wash the tomatoes, peel and cut into small pieces.
2. Clean and chop the hare. Set aside.
3. Put a paella pan on the heat with a little olive oil and, when hot, add the onion and pepper. Add salt and pepper and sauté for 10 minutes.
4. Add the tomato and let it release all the juice. Then add the rice and hare. Season again. When the meat begins to brown, pour in the chicken stock and simmer on a medium heat for 20 minutes until the rice is ready and the stock has evaporated.
5. When the rice is cooked and the stock evaporated, add the strands of saffron and stir so the rice takes on colour. Remove from heat and leave to stand for 5 minutes before serving.

Note

The rice used in this recipe is characterized as being three to five times longer than wide and does not stick so easily. But we must bear in mind that, due to its high amylose content, this type of rice requires longer cooking time than the rest. Basmati, Jasmine or Ferrini are examples of long grain rice.

Rice Dishes

Ampurdan-style Rice

Ingredients:

FOR 6 PEOPLE
DIFFICULTY: LOW
TIME: 1 HOUR

500 g rice
200 g squid
200 g pork ribs
1 l water
12 mussels
4 prawns
4 Norway lobsters
4 fresh sausages
2 ripe tomatoes
2 onions
2 cloves of garlic
extra virgin olive oil
a few sprigs of parsley
salt

Preparation:

1. Put a paella pan on the heat with a little olive oil, and when hot, sauté the prawns and lobsters. When they start to brown, remove them from the pan and set aside.
2. Dice the squid into small cubes and the sausages into very small pieces. In the same oil, sauté the pork ribs, the squid and the sausages. When everything is ready, remove from heat and set aside.
3. Peel the onions and garlic, and finely chop. Wash, peel and grate the tomatoes. Chop the parsley.
4. Put the onion into the pan and sauté 15 minutes over a low heat. Once it is well browned, add the garlic and parsley together with the grated tomato. Sauté about 5 minutes before adding the rice. Stir well and pour in the water.
5. Add the prawns and lobsters to the pan, as well as the squid, pork ribs and sausages that had been previously set aside. Correct the seasoning and cook over a high heat for about 12 minutes.
6. Add the mussels and cook for about 6 or 7 minutes more.
7. Remove the rice from the heat and leave to stand for 5 minutes before serving.

Rice with **Lobster**

Ingredients:

FOR 6 PEOPLE
DIFFICULTY: MEDIUM
TIME: 1 HOUR AND 15 MINUTES

400 g round-grain rice
2.5 kg lobster
2 l water
1 onion
2 tomatoes
1 green pepper
1.5 kg of rockfish
350 g crabs
4 cloves of garlic
2 sprigs parsley
extra virgin olive oil
salt

Preparation:

1. Peel and chop the onion; wash the pepper, remove the seeds and chop; peel and chop two cloves of garlic. Put a paella pan on the heat with a dash of olive oil and sauté these three ingredients over a low heat for about 10 minutes, stirring often.
2. Meanwhile, wash and grate the tomatoes and, when the sauce is ready, add them. Continue cooking 5 minutes more.
3. After this time, pour the sauce in a large saucepan and add the clean rockfish, crabs and water. Let the stock cook for 30 minutes with the pan uncovered. When it is ready, strain it and set it aside, hot.
4. While the stock is cooking, cut the lobster tails into regular pieces and the heads in half lengthwise. Set aside.
5. Put the same paella pan where the sauce was on the heat with a dash of olive oil and fry the lobster legs. Take them out when they are well cooked.
6. In the same oil, sauté the parsley with the remaining garlic, also chopped, stirring constantly for a couple of minutes. While stirring, add the rice and sauté about 3 minutes, until the rice has absorbed the oil from making the sauce.
7. Pour the stock over the rice, covering it, and cook for 5 minutes over a high heat. After this time, add the lobster heads and tails. Lower the heat and cook another 10 minutes, until the rice is ready.
8. Correct the seasoning if necessary, take the paella pan off the heat and leave to stand 3 minutes before serving.

Baked **Octopus** Rice

Ingredients:

FOR 6 PEOPLE
DIFFICULTY: MEDIUM
TIME: 1 HOUR

500 g rice
800 g octopus
1 onion
extra virgin olive oil
1 spoonful of sweet paprika
pepper
salt

Preparation:

1. Clean the octopus, removing guts, eyes and mouth. Rinse thoroughly under cold running water and then blanch it in boiling, slightly salted water, in a covered saucepan, for 20 minutes.
2. After this time, turn off the heat and leave the octopus in the stock. When cool, drain (setting aside the cooking stock) and cut into small pieces.
3. Return to heat the stock over low heat and set aside, because it will be used later, but keep it warm.
4. Peel and chop the onion. Put a pan (preferably with a lid and oven-proof) on the heat with three or four tablespoons of olive oil and, when it is hot, sauté the onion slowly. Add the octopus pieces with a pinch of salt and pepper, and stir so that it absorbs the flavour.
5. Add the paprika and a couple of spoonfuls of the octopus cooking stock. Cover the pan and leave to cook, slowly adding more stock, always soft heat and with the pan covered, until the octopus is tender.
6. Pour in the rest of the cooking stock together with ½ l of hot water and bring to the boil. Preheat oven to 160 ° C.
7. Add the rice to the pan, check the seasoning, and stir. Take the pan off the heat, and put it, covered, into the oven and leave it there until the rice absorbs the liquid.
8. Finally, remove the pan from the oven, drizzle with a little oil and serve.

The **Gentleman's** Rice

Ingredients:

FOR 6 PEOPLE
DIFFICULTY: MEDIUM
TIME: 1 HOUR AND 15 MINUTES

500 g Bomba rice
150 g prawns
200 g King prawns
100 g canned razor clams
200 g boneless fish, chopped
250 g boneless chicken thighs
100 g fresh peas, shelled
1.5 l water
1 ripe tomato
2 cloves of garlic
1 green pepper
1 glass of white wine
extra virgin olive oil
a few strands of saffron
salt

Preparation:

1. Peel the prawns and King prawns; set aside the tails.
2. Pour the water into a pan and, when it starts to boil, add the prawn and King prawn shells and heads. Cook for 30 minutes over a high heat. After this time, strain the stock and set aside. More or less 750 ml of stock is required to make the rice.
3. Pour water into another pan to cook the peas; when ready, drain and set aside.
4. Finely chop the garlic and dice the washed pepper. Peel and grate the tomato. Chop the chicken meat.
5. Put a paella pan on the heat with a dash of oil and, when it is hot, fry the garlic. After 5 minutes, remove the garlic and brown the chicken in the same oil, to seal it on all sides. Then put it on the edge of the pan and sauté the pepper and tomato.
6. To complete the rice sauce, raise the heat, pour in the white wine and wait for it to evaporate; then add the rice by drawing a band in the centre of the pan. Scatter it across the surface and cook it for a couple minutes over a high heat. Then add the stock, fish and saffron, check the seasoning and simmer until the rice is nearly ready.
7. 5 minutes before the rice is fully cooked, add the prawns, King prawns, razor clam and peas. Stir.
8. Remove the pan from the heat and allow the rice to rest 5 minutes covered with a cloth before serving.

Note

The birthplace of this delicious dish was Barcelona, at the end of the 19th century and it is known by various names: Parellada Rice, Parellada Paella and The Gentleman's Rice. Juli Parellada, a refined Barcelona dandy of the time, often visited Café El Suizo, where one day he asked the waiter to serve him a rice dish in a somewhat peculiar way: he wanted all the fish or meat to be added without any bones, so he could enjoy it without any "interruptions". The dish became so popular that many elegant restaurants in the city decided to include The Gentleman's Rice on their sophisticated menus.

Murcia-style Stewed Rice

Ingredients:

FOR 6 PEOPLE
DIFFICULTY: HIGH
TIME: 1 HOUR AND 30 MINUTES

500 g rice
2 kg of varied fish
(mullet, bream, whitebait)
2 l water
200 g fresh prawns
400 g ripe tomatoes
200 ml olive oil
8 cloves of garlic
4 dried peppers (ñoras)
6 sprigs of parsley
a few strands of saffron
pepper
salt

Preparation:

1. Clean the fish and slice thickly; Set aside the heads. Peel four cloves of garlic. Clean the dried peppers and remove the seeds. Wash, peel and chop the tomatoes. Chop the parsley.
2. Put a large pan on the heat and add half of the oil. When it is hot, fry the peppers. When well fried, remove them and put them in a mortar. Add the four cloves of garlic and mash everything. Set aside.
3. In the same oil, fry the fish heads, then remove them and set aside. Add chopped tomatoes and fry for 5 minutes. Add the water, parsley and the pepper and garlic mixture; leave to cook for 5 minutes more.
4. In that stock, cook the (seasoned) fish with the fried heads and a few strands of saffron. Once cooked, remove the fish from the stock and set aside in a bowl. Discard the heads.
5. Take a cup of stock from the pan and set aside; pour the remaining stock over the rice and cook for 20 minutes over a low heat; correct the seasoning if necessary and stir from time to time. A few minutes before it is ready, add the prawns.
6. Mash two cloves of garlic in a mortar and add the cup of stock that had been set aside; mix well and pour over the fish.
7. Prepare a garlic sauce by mashing the two remaining cloves of garlic and slowly adding 100 ml of oil, while beating until the sauce thickens.
8. The rice and fish are served separately: the rice as the first course, then the fish with the garlic sauce as the second.

Sailor's Pepper Rice

Ingredients:

FOR 6 PEOPLE
DIFFICULTY: MEDIUM
TIME: 1 HOUR

400 g rice
500 g mussels
250 g cuttlefish
100 g prawns
2 tomatoes
4 cloves of garlic
1 green pepper
1 onion
extra virgin olive oil
1 l water
a few strands of saffron
chopped parsley
pepper
salt

Preparation:

1. Peel and cut the onion and garlic. Wash and chop the tomatoes and peppers.
2. Put a paella pan on the heat with a dash of oil, a little saffron and parsley. When the oil is hot, add the onion and the garlic and, once they are browned, add the tomato, pepper chopped cuttlefish and the prawns.
3. Sauté all together a couple of minutes. Then add the water and simmer for 15 minutes.
4. Meanwhile, put a frying pan on the heat with a little oil and add the mussels; brown them gently and discard the ones that don't open. Add the open ones to the paella pan where the stock is cooking and simmer a few more minutes.
5. When the stock boils, add the rice. Then the salt and pepper, and cook until the rice is almost ready, between 15 and 20 minutes.
6. Before serving, take paella pan off the heat, cover and leave to stand about 5 minutes.

Note

Traditionally, this Sailor's Rice should be eaten with a wooden spoon and directly from the pan. It has to be quite soupy. You can add more or less pepper according to taste. However, don't add too little, as the pepper enhances the flavours.

Rice Stews

Ibérico Pork Tenderloin

Ingredients:

FOR 4 PEOPLE
DIFFICULTY: LOW
TIME: 45 MINUTES

400 g round-grain rice
50 ml olive oil
2 cloves of garlic
½ onion
1 green pepper
½ red pepper
1 tomato
300 g pork tenderloin
1 l vegetable stock
4 slices of toast
salt

Preparation:

1. Peel and chop the onion. Wash the peppers, remove seeds and chop into small cubes. Peel the garlic. Wash and chop the tomato.
2. Put a pan on the heat with the oil and fry onion until transparent. Add the garlic and sauté 1 minute more. Add the peppers and tomato and simmer for 10 minutes or until the sauce is ready.
3. Clean and dice the pork into small cubes and add it to the sauce. Leave to cook for 15 minutes, stirring occasionally.
4. Pour in the stock and, when is hot, add the rice and simmer for 20 minutes.
5. Check the rice and add salt to taste. If necessary, cook a few more minutes.
6. Serve on individual plates with a slice of toast.

Note

Loin is the tastiest and juiciest part of the Ibérico pig. It stands out for its high protein. Per 100 g, it has only 158 calories, 22.3 g protein, 7.6 g fat and no carbohydrates.

Chicken & **Spinach** Rice Stew

Ingredients:

FOR 6 PEOPLE
DIFFICULTY: LOW
TIME: 45 MINUTES

500 g rice
400 g chicken
300 ml white wine
1.5 l chicken stock
40 g crushed tomatoes
4 cloves of garlic
4 handfuls of fresh spinach
1 onion
1 roasted pepper
paprika
extra virgin olive oil
salt

Preparation:

1. Peel and chop the onion. Peel and slice the garlic. Bone and dice the chicken; season.
2. Wash the spinach well and drain in a colander. Set aside.
3. Sauté the onion in a frying pan with a dash of oil and a pinch of salt. After about 3 minutes, add the garlic, tomato and chicken meat. Raise the heat and stir until chicken is golden brown.
4. Add the rice to the frying pan, sauté a little and then add the spinach and white wine. Salt to taste if necessary, add a pinch of paprika and let the wine evaporate for 2 minutes over a low heat.
5. Pour the stock over the rice, cover, and simmer over a low heat for 15 minutes.
6. Turn off the heat, leave to stand for 2 minutes and serve the stew with roasted pepper cut into strips.

Note

The rice stew in this recipe is a very tasty, complete and easy-to-prepare dish, ideal to enjoy as a family meal. Although the taste of spinach is unique, the stew can also be made with chard, which must be previously chopped. The result will be just as good.

Gypsy Rice Stew

Ingredients:

FOR 6 PEOPLE
DIFFICULTY: LOW
TIME: 1 HOUR AND 10 MINUTES

500 g rice
250 g lamb neck
100 g lean pork
100 g pork ribs
1.5 l beef stock
100 g green beans
2 potatoes
1 onion
2 tomatoes
1 red pepper
extra virgin olive oil
a few strands of saffron
salt

Preparation:

1. Peel and finely chop the onion. Wash the peppers, remove seeds and cut into strips. Wash the green beans and chop up. Peel and chop the tomatoes. Peel, wash and dice the potatoes into small pieces.
2. Chop all the meat.
3. Put a frying pan on the heat, add a few strands of saffron, heat them and then crush them in a mortar. Set aside.
4. Put a saucepan on the heat with a dash of oil and, when it is hot, add all the meat and brown it for 10 minutes over a medium heat, stirring occasionally.
5. Next, gradually add the vegetables; first the onion, then the pepper, then the green beans and potatoes. Stir and sauté for about 2 minutes.
6. Add the tomato. Stir and sauté for 2 or 3 minutes more.
7. Pour in the beef stock and simmer for 20 minutes over a medium heat. After this time, add the rice and the crushed saffron, and cook 15 minutes more. Correct the seasoning if necessary and remove from the heat.

Rabbit, Cumin & Clove Rice Stew

Ingredients:

FOR 6 PEOPLE
DIFFICULTY: LOW
TIME: 1 HOUR

500 g rice
1 rabbit
400 g tomatoes
75 g sweet roasted peppers
500 ml white wine
1.5 l chicken stock
100 ml extra virgin olive oil
½ teaspoon ground red pepper
1/2 teaspoon of cumin
3 grains of black pepper
2 bay leaves
a few strands of saffron
coarse salt
3 cloves
2 cloves of garlic

Preparation:

1. Wash, peel, and crush the tomatoes; set aside in a bowl. Peel and slice the garlic cloves. Chop the rabbit and set aside the liver. Wash the peppers and cut them into strips.
2. Crush the spices and salt in the mortar.
3. Put a pan on the heat with a dash of oil and, when it is hot, sauté the garlic, rabbit and liver for 15 or 20 minutes.
4. Once the rabbit is ready, add the crushed tomatoes and continue cooking for 15 minutes from when they start to simmer. Then pour in the wine and stock.
5. When the stock starts to boil, add the pepper strips, the crushed spices and the bay leaves. Stir.
6. Add the rice and cook over a medium heat for 20 minutes.
7. Serve immediately to avoid the rice absorbing too much liquid.

Note

The spices take centre stage in this recipe. They mix perfectly with the rice, because despite being a food with very little flavour, the grain absorbs all the aromas of the other ingredients, and more even if they are strong spices like cumin and cloves as in this recipe.

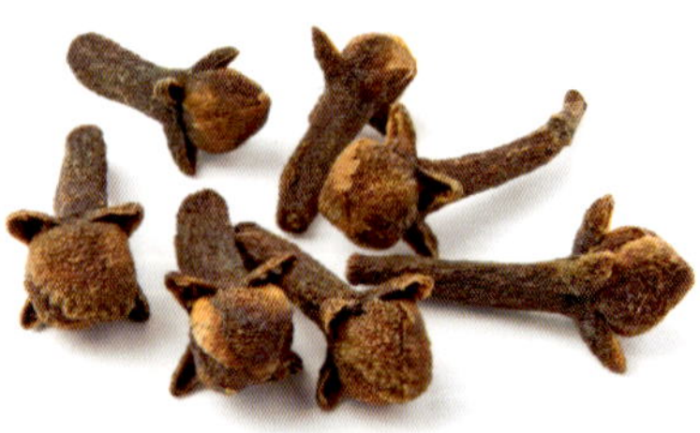

ALPHABETICAL INDEX OF RECIPES

Translated by Carole Patton
Layout: Natalia Rodríguez

C/ Campezo, 13 - 28022 Madrid
Tel.: 91 3009100 - Fax: 91 3009118

D.L.: M-35946-MMXI